Snowflakes and Ashes

by

orde

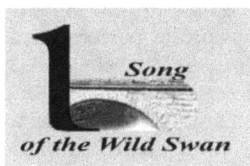

Published by Song, 2014.
Song is an Imprint of:
Song of the Wild Swan Ltd.
1 Folly Bridge, Oxford, OX1 4LB, UK.
www.songwildswan.com
tel +44 (0) 1865 240572
fax +44 (0) 1865 246565
e: info@songwildswan.com

Snowflakes and Ashes by orde
ISBN 9781909777170

First published: c.1980's, Private printing, (6 copies).
eBook and Book: 2014 Song, Oxford.

Acknowledgements

Song eBook Design series by Laurence Hutton-Smith.
Cover Design: Laurence Hutton-Smith.
Cover Image: from photo, courtesy of morguefile.com
Book Production: Amaury Marinho Junior

Contents

Snowflakes
                    and

                                        Ashes

Words

            candles
two of them,
after   dinner
        tandberg
a
 n
  d   Quad.
t a p e s

                    Pertsovka

                                        and you're old enough
                                        to reap pain
                                        and young enough
                                        to sell.

a
 n
  d   t h o u

WELL   I dreamed
I   dreamed
            dreamed

and   still ; still   and
    even   even
words   words   words

                                        look at mother intellect
                                        on the run

look
         a
          t f
             a
              t
               h
                e
                 r   heart

on the run.

   n
  d   I
a

     was

thinking thinking

    about
and even still and even still.

weLL I d
         r
          e
           a
            m
             e
              d   t   t h o u g h t
                    I

w   r s   o   d f y
 o d   c u l   l

could

f   y   f   y
 l   l

                    to
the sun.
oh   yes   its

a
  l
    o
      v
        e
          p
            o
              e
                m
as one 15 year old
told me;
l o v e   was   something   terrible
he s
      a
        w what   it   did   to   his   friends.
oh

                    yes

                              its

                              soothed
                              beneath the
                              artists loving mind.

into words.
mere words
just words.
words.

i n   t h e   s h a d o w   o f   g o^D   d o
I w e e p.

                              blessed are
                              the tears

relations.the blood;
parents .

w   ee   p   ing   wide
wide.

ah   well

                              the ending of this
                              tale

is just m a k i n g   it

alone

                              oranges and lemons
                              oranges and lemons

s a n g t h e b e l l s ,

just   when   you
    when
    were
    told;
    he said
sh ak ing   my   hand   off.
                    jesus was a saviour
    a
     n
      d he p
               o
                u
                 r
                  s
d
 o
  w
   n
                    like honey.
                    amongst the garbage.

    he said
as the re w as   a l e a   n   i   ng
    out   for   snowflakes   and love.

                    I am a simple man

never been
  w
   i
    s
     h   i   c
                o
                 u
                  l
                   d

    see
  your eyes
    look
    into
    your
    eyes
and in your eyes
        i
    see
spinning around
 ah well

                    the ending of this tale

is j u s t the making
            of it
alone. as words. just words.

D O N ' T

       philosophise
         o r
       P O E T I S E

                             lovebirds are talking

lovebirds are walking
in our eyes.

                             are they telling lies.

L O O K
       into his eyes
       p r o g r a m m e d
       not to   see

look into his eyes.   *are they telling lies.*

have you seen the

   e
         y   e   s

w ith

  his   worn   out   wornout.
sold.
  and   he   says   there
            is

NO SHINING
N O   L I G H T
I   N

         eyes
and he says
   there is
     n
     o

s sun g
 h i i
  n

and he says

   the
    s
    u
    n
does not shine for me

and I say for you

                that
the eyes
              shine

d i d
 and

 do

let   me lead   you
      by   the   hand

to the promissed land

eye   i   eye
            n

my father promissed me

            t
            h
            a
            t
          h e
         would
          buy
           a

         house
           o
           r
        that part
        li ke
            m
            y
        brot   hers
            a
            l
            w
            a
            y
            s

        d
          r
            e
              a   m
                      s

     f
  o   t   a   u
         h t h o   s
                      e

and I live in

a m s t e r d a m
        now.

and I speak a language I can never
language I can
never sing.

and watch the setting sun

i   u r
 n o
ey es
setting
  sun
i   u
 n o u
ey es
setting

ag in
  a

there's never much to say
to talkabout
to say it aloud

A lou D.
 b
 u
 t
say
 i
 t

ANYWAY.

before and after
from seeing to believing
I've seen the future

it is not b l e e d i n g
is it   ?
                         and
it was a g o o d eye
          a
       good
       eye
         t
         h
         e
         n
                         and

    now
a goodeaeye
       a
        y
         e

  o t
     c
      o
       m
        e

 t
  h
   e
    r
    e,
       s the r
                u
                 b.

 t n all I remember t
  he   h
                       e
                       r
                       e
    was this band
      of two
      to play.
  this   evening
  this   night
     that
  ni g ht

    was a ni
             g
             ht

     to
  remember

to
 recall
  to
   believe
                          it
  to

                    l ov e

let's not bleed   the lines.
                  between

                                        never fool myself

               that I
                 was
                 dreaming.

 we   we
   looked   loved.

     wouldn't   you:

                                        time and time again

 a
  g a
     i n   a g a i
               n   a
                                        time and time again

      again
                                        another picture

    on the
          W   A   L   L
   the wall
    calls and c   a   l   l   s
 a
  g a
     i n.
 i
 ._ r e c a l l a l l t h o s e

 consolations.

                                        keep on going to the limit

               o v e r f
                          l
                            o   w

tothelimit

you
know.
know.

now
now .

there's n⁰ ₒother pˡᵃᶜe
tᵒ gₒ

                                        to the limit here we go.

p   a   u   s   e

to slow - can't
        staⁿd
        the pace:

                                        do it nice and easy

do it
  no
do what I
  have not to do.
we saw it all
ALL
with our two own eyes.
Aeye.
  ʰ   ʰ
hⁱ ᵍ hⁱ ᵍ   oh so high

                                        so rich so beautiful

r e a l i t y

                                        of a saint and a bedroom

golden   palms
      coconut

earth   heaven
      and

on top of the world

high high oh at22 so high

so beautiful

in the eye.

its not so unwise to fast

til

heigh l

to such h

to l o v e you

you high

so high

in the eye.

All the words of wisdom

would agree.

t h a t

snow flakes

angels in pale grey

my story is quite

ordinary

one thing I'll say for me
I was not doing nothing

just t a n d

s i n g about

I was not doing nothing

just i t t

s ing about

just s t a n d i n g and it s

```
                      G
   i'm   A    N            E        S
                             L
   brother
                                        I was not doing nothing

       just      standing     about

 in  t h   o   t h  t                    
        i s r  om   i s s udio

       begining
                  and
                     end

                                        screaming in the night.

                   O
             B
   l ying A              U        T

                                        I was not doing nothing

     jus      talking     about
        t
                                        that's all I was doing
   w          i    e
   e      s p  r it  d
   LL          i
     along

   w    t
   e  j us  sit            about
      j
         eyeing

   s t r a  i   g   h   t    totha

                             heart
   cool and beautful
   firely and light
   just right.
   smiles  of joy.
   no time   l   i    k    e

              the present.
```

(

t

i

m

j   e

u

m

p

)

thanks for the drink fellah
am going hom e now.

blowing in the wind.

s   a

   c   t   t   e   r   e d

searching
      for   the

           madness

   of

l   o   v   e

for I long for the dry land
of your shores.

gottah go hom e now he says.

feeling for where his

heart was h
         u
          n
          g.

just a creature looking
for a little piece.

and loo k   oor
    s   next   d

persons.

            b
             ack
through sthe   wall.
       air and
u p s t   a l
           l

I was screaming at the night.

I mean   door.
   next

       il y a un mot qui m'exalte, un mot
       que je n'ai jamais entendu sans
       ressentir un grand frisson, un grand
       espoir:le plus grand,celui de vaincre les
       puissances de ruine et de mort qui
       accablent les hommes,ce mot c'est:

je t'aime.

```
hands  b r  ush   ing   a
                          side.
next door again.
that floor again.
that room again.
that wall again.

         A                    man
              says
            I must  leave
t  o  lea  ve   y  ou    t   wo
t  o  tal   k    it
       a      it
        bout

in    the   human      war
```

I was screaming at the night.

```
you gotta understand
    gee
        y    ou      ta
                  got
                        u
                         n
                          d
                           e
                            r stand
                               stand
        i  t
         s
      it      was
        .not
         m
         y
       fault.
you understand.
```

deep down there is good.

gee somehow I was had
you gotta understand

```
    my daddy is where I stay
    univer     sit        y
    yes   shouldn't
        i            be
       here  now.
```

b ut h ey ,   he-y   ,   he   I
h e^y h e_y

  its
not that
  I'm
  you
   h
   a
   v
   e

*the trouble is that no-one
wants a fellah with a social
disease.*

ooh   ooh
   ooh

   try
it again   just next door.
    in
       a   few

       minutes.
I know   I know

    I know
we just
    looked   there.

there   looked
   sat.
   still.
   looked.

           no movement.
exchanged eyes.

       exchanged I's.
exchanged   ayes.

this time now
the look in your eyes
were just a little
different.

      I think.

you
        talked
      this time.

you   moved
                                 this time.
     this time now.

just   when   you
               feel

               wordless.

                                        love will find you

     talking   with

          our eyes.

          silently

          so   long

                                        I can't remember

               our eyes

in our   hearts.

                                        so long I can't remember
                                        that old look that old look
                                        of love

          so   long
               you

can't   remember

and we saw
          we saw
               we say we say we saw

          we were

          seeing.

                                        that old book of love

                    uₚ there
hey you   uₚ
                         wₐke uₚ
                         will
                              yₒu
                              here
gₒ   re
 ᵒDwake up   ᵒu   up tʰ
     willyᵒu   up tʰ

a ey
ae
ye

up   there.

please

a
little while
longer
in
my
heart

please just
a

little

while   longer

in
my
heart
please.

just that little old look

of love of love

that old look

love

p
e
e
t.
talking is so s

one

can   take one's   time
    ones time
            looking

                                    someone who is always there

    someone
    tell   me   its a
                                game.

how i wish i
    i wish i   could just p
                            l
                            a
                            y
                            one
                                more
            and I know
                        i will
                                n
                                e
                                v
                                e
                                r

                        see

        again

                                    it's the nature of the game

    time   time
        and
                        again

                                    it's a fool's game

            f   l
             oo
            b e
             w
             a
             r
             e   's

                                    coming into dry land

for I long to touch
                    the
                        nature
                            of
                                the g
                                     ame

        t i m e   and   t i m e
                a a
                 g i n

taking

    our   t i m e
       how   our

        eyes

just   loooked

    $i_{k_{now}}$
    $i_{k_{now}}$
    i
      saw
    $i_{k_{now}}$

its to be the nature of the game

here I am sitting in the game.

playing on the nature.

of my mind.

oh poor thing.

                        its a brand new sight

in my light..

    its gods wi^{ll}to be seen.

        in   light.

wrong place to be in

        from begining to end.

a   bit

    of both
    actually.

a   rise

fire li^gh^t.

    as_b_r_i_g_h_t
                          moving.

       all

the words the words

                      the shadows of your heart

  and its b   l a

         z i

              ng

    your heart apart.

into the wide eyes of your heart.

c
o
m
i
n
g
back
a
g
a
i
n

y   ou
      asked me
           afterwards
all innocently
      like a child
I can hear your voice saying it all
    so
  loud
    all

clear   clear

did you   see

            yourself

            in me

                                        oh all the words of wisdom

oh wisdom worlds.

oh worlds oh

                        whatever.

in the eye of the beholder.

                                        and

    dd e
 s u   n l y

        i

                    dis s
                        a
                          peared.

            I mean
            who
            wants
                to
            say the
            words

                o
                f

            love.

say the words of love

and
            you came by after me.   t h i n k
            concerned for me.   i

i think.

                    who

knows.

        why.

the reason why

                    who
knows.

                        for me.
oh you
    w
     o
      r
       l
        d
         s of wisdom
        w
         o
          r
           l
            d
             s of wisdom
        w
         o
          r
           d
            s of wisdom

                    the h
                         a
                          n
                           d
        that pushed these
                          w
                           o
                            r
                             l
                              d
                               s of wisdom
                                          a
                                          s
                                          i
                                          d
                                          e.

                                front page story

that yes.
        its true.
                our love is true.
no place.

                                sure we had some good times

        then

with our eyes
            see my face
        now

he looks scared like a rabbit.
no I can't go.

let go.   lets go.

   so soon

lets go.   let go.

it does not feel right tonight

worlds of wisdom in our eyes that night.

f   e   e   l

the

force

f   e   e   l

the

force

between us.

f   l   w   i

o   n   g

all night

between us.

eye   to   eye

with the stars and the moon
in our eyes tonight
in our eyes tonight.

               there

          was

     the

whole w_o_r_l_d

        I

           mean

   in

our eyes tonight.

      was

   me   and

      you

in our eyes tonight.

    t o n i g h t.

it was so right
it was so bright
it was just so

    i_n our s uⁿ

   t h i s   n i g h t
   t h i s to n i g h t

it was really big.
god it was big.
   really big.

m_e   and   e^y_e

in our eyes tonight

think

of

all the right words   down   tonight.

it was so bright tonight.

tonight tonight

not

special

he whispers.

have a flight to   catch .
                        he says.

no sight.
goodnight.
no me and
  you to
    night.

                this time
                this time.

no.
flight
    to night.
so slight
    that sight. tonight.
            no light
                so bright.

just

a

                   light.
tonight.
          sleep tight. goodnight.

this time
this time
     this night

              it

was made in

heaven

                         not in hell.

oh GoD
          this time tonight.

that light
that light
     this sight
   this world of light.
thatnight.
     that heaven.

this time tonight.

it was made
it was made
made.

                    have to go you said.
        you felt sad.

you cried.
     oh gOd you cried.
you felt.
you felt.
felt.

it

was I supposed to BELIEVE.

that you really did NOT   love

            really

                    me.

            really

                    love

                                me.

those   TEARS

        you   cried.

                        burst

        my   eardrums.

that I really could not   hear.

            . so
                s
                 a
                  d
                   t
                    h
                     a
                      t
                       n
                        i
                         g
                          h
                           t.

love   me

                                    was I supposed to believe

that

you REALLY

loved me.

oh wow ohwow its hard.

god its hard

tears flying across.

in sight.

right

across the sky.
windowed soul

will you not come home with me.
we can make all right.

all night.

everything
all
right.
in the coldest height.

i must gottah go you say.
i don't want to leave like this you say.

picture it.

what a night.
everything all right.
gottah go you say.

i will
   be there
        not
          to be
             with you
                you'll see.

      in   the

                 empty
                 h
                 e
                 a
                 r
                 t
                 s
     so cold
            with light.

is that   is it that you really love me.
     the way you really
                  love me.
       being
            h
             e
              r e
                 t
                  h
                   e
                    r
                     e
         wise one c
                   o
                    m
                     e
                      in.
you worlds of wisdom.

    tell me tell him

is it   what I'm supposed to believe
     really
    that
        yo u love me .
back   and   forth
     cards   spread
          out.
or
     at
          least
those on the table.
cards

cards
that love has played.
to fool whom.

you can't deal them again

your heart

is

full

o
f

hands

a
n
d

your
hands

f
u
l
l

hearts.   of

s
h   o
c
s
h
a
k   ing

you can't deal them again

you
know.

you

know

i

stay.   can't

you   and

s
h
u
f
f
l
e

b
a
c
k

again.

to
  deal   the cards   again.
to
  change
     the
          suite.

but you can't deal 'em again

                  P
P   i   ck 'em   u
   P u t   'em down.
p   i   c   k 'em up
  p
      u   t   'em d o
                     w
                    n.
a   g   i
          a   n
      a
      n
      D
a
           a   n.
    g   i

l

  o

  v

  e   g
        g
        e   s back a
                    n
                    d
 forth.   in
           a
     b   n
             d
   o
   f l o v e. s

```
w                    n          l
          i                     o
                                s
                                e
l        o        s        e      w
                                  i
                                  n

      deal        'em              again
Y                                      
 o                    Y
  u  can't d  al the   o       l the
           e            u  can't d
                                  e
              a
              eyes
Y                                     n.
 o                          who      a
  u  can't d  al them          th  ag
           e                     em
w
 e
  ll  so it                    goes

              on

t        s    s  t  r    e    a    m        s
 e
  a
   r

b      u      r      s      t


              f
              a
              c        s
                       s
              e        e
               l

                        wordless.
s
 o
  b s. from the heart.
the

          mind       s         e
                 .             y
                               e  had  s
                                       e
                                       e
                                       n.
the
          heart      s         t
                               e
                               a
                               r  had  f
                                       e
                                       l
                                       t.

          and
   seeing        feeling.
```

                        lo
                          v
                          es

      back
                                        p
                                         ack.
      e   i
       v   a   h
        e
         r
          y   once in   w
                                l
                                 e.
      YOU
          j   r
           u   b
            s
             t   s
                     u   t
                                 into tears.

      feeling how much I must

         MUST
                  be

                      made   to

         suffer

                  because

                  of the love
      o
      f
      YOU.

      You
        felt
             on

                  my behalf.
                  be half.

      knowing   what
                the   law o
                                f
                                   the
      lal
         aa
           l
            aa
                                 was
                                   a
                                   yin
                                      g

      YOUR   HEART
            was   saying..

                  again.

      a b u r s t of t e a r s

sobbs

shaking

your

bod y

provoking

equal

amounts

in

me.

how

else could it be.   half and half.

well so   it   goes on.

                              y
                              o
                              u
                        r

                    heart
                 was
            saying
         y
         o
         u
         r
            heard-h
                  e
                  a
                  r
                  t was saying

I

        must   le
                    ave i
                        t

I

        don't   l

                 o

                 v

                 e

you.

            oh

                        tears

b u r   s   t   i   n   g
  r
      e   like
         a   tears
t
h   k
e   i

s   n
o
b breaks out   g
        burst.

i know

    in my

heart

    how sad it
    how sad it

    will be

for you

        what you

   will have

      to go

through.

       thinking

  of what

        you'll

have to go through.

thinking of what you'll have to go through.

   oh
      the
tears

   come

      to my eyes.

eyes.

          h
           u
            l
             l
              o.

                do I have to go
                                t
                                 o
                                  o.

dear love.
          dear gOd

                    d
                     e
                      a
                       r
                          god
                               o
                                f love.

STAY   AWHILE LONGER.

                        LOVE.

no

            not love
            just STAY

don't say.

DON'T

               DO

STAY   AWHILE LONGER

                    A LITTLE LONGER
AND GUARD LOVE.

no.

      not guard.
      just stay.

       LOVE.

stay longer.

      NO NOT LONGER.

      JUST.

           one

more time.

           time.

              nothing lasts for long

YOU SAY

      nothing.

              nothing lasts for long

     GONE

NO   not nothing.
NO   not gone.

     MY HEART

MY HEART.

in my heart, in my heart

above me.

          no MOVEMENT

             JUST.

OUT.

            still.

no not out.

          not still.

              everything.
seing me seeing me.must have been a funny sight.
NOT FUNNY.

      just.

something in my

EYE.

           IN MY HEART.

        IN MY SOUL.

IN MY BODY.

          everywhere and no where.
all and all.

they'll have to carry me out.

                              oh woe.
WOE.

        too MUCH.

                                    time.
time when we were in our eyes.

            WHO KNOWS THIS FEELING.
this EXCHANGE.

          no not EXchange.
  THIS FLOW.

            uncalled for , unasked.

      JUST.

LOVE TO LOVE.

me to you , you to me.

                        aeye beyond words.
settle.

STAY STAY OH FEELINGS.
                        stay/
JUST STAY A WHILE.

quietness descend.

beauty grow.

ah yes

picture a room.

all there
but nothing
except

that feeling.

GROW.

smile.

open up the EYES to your heart

Grow HEART

GROW.

MORNING SUN

fade.

I want to see again.

can't deal 'em again   .

stay OH GLIMPSES.

of what   of what.
it was.

IT IS SUFFICIENT.

IT IS all   there ever IS.

life love joy.

wisdom truth right action.

            REAL.

heaven.

GOD SPED THE LOVE.

                    at the time.

aye.

    that it did.

                    BACK AND FORTH.

one

    BROWN SOFT AND YELLOW EYE.

he SMILED
                YES HE SMILED.

simultaneously.

                WHEN I SMILED.

like flowers opening up to bloom.

            one could not help smiling.

perfectly matched

            AT

                THE GROWTH.

            PERFECTLY MATCHED.

ALL THROUGH OUR EYES.

not a word.

not a movement.

light just light

forces beyond

heaven

not just love

light of the great blaze

you gods of wisdom

you know what

IT IS

IT

IS

ALL ABOUT

ALL ABOUT

Smile to smile.

feeling to feeling.

growth to growth

oh

point to point.

just .
love runs fast .
fast.

ladies man , *ladies man*

so cold,so cold.

couldn't

be just

friends.

dope.

unbelievable
unbelievable.

we gone and fall in love.
just had.
no words nothing but.
just.
and

this axe falls.

right..

right in the middle.

unbelievable

dope.

TA CHA NICE GAME.
no

not
even that.
NO.

JUST NOTHING.?

LIFE MOVES ON.

HO HO

NOT LIFE.
not that
not that
AXE MOVES ON.
wanted to.
AXE AXE.

says
GOING
to give you my very best.

AND

SMASH

                    open your heart.
                      wham bang
                            thankyou

                                              unbelievable
            you do you do

                              you axe.

                    RIGHT THROUGH   *unbelievable*
                  heart , tart , who cares.

                    JUST THUMP.

                      thump
                                              unbelievable
              no more no more by my side .
                      i just had to
                had to
                        just
                  collapse.

    wham bang.
                        you you

                                axe.

    HEART
          head.
              IN TWO.
                    WHAM.

    JUST LIKE THAT.

                    no problem,

    HELL.
      its unbelievable

              just words.

          BACK
              to
                EARTH.

                    back to normal.
                hey

        CAUSE MY HEART

                                            ladies man, ladies man

                you must
                    LEAVE.
        leave,

                                            ladies man ladies man

            Will bOy
                will

                    POWER

            it takes say as you will.
            it takes feeling.

                wow man.

        IT

    to say that.

                i love you.
        it takes
          it takes.

                FEELING
                    I say that it takes
                    feeling to say that

    I LOVE YOU.

    and feel it.

                    SEE

                        it.
                            being it.
                    it can be so hard to find
                a light in these dark nights.

        aye aye.

    EARTH

            aye.
        in these dark nights.

RAZZLE DAZZLE.

I'M TOLD
who tells me so.

I know.

now.

THAT.
well.

I'm Told .

it
is
impossible
or is it/was it
possible.

plane désespérément d'aile

that love

cannot be seen.

I

mean I think I mean   I think it should

BE FELT.

don't you.

you could escape.

You could keep cool.

I WAS OUT.

proverbial light

LIGHT.

my
  heart

        on the floor.

                  just keep cool.

            stay cool.
      such a heavy sight.

                  right out .
              right out he goes.
  right out.
          right out.

                        on
                    the floor

                  IS

  keep
      cool.

              keep cool.

                    cooling

  right on the floor.

                        cool fire.

  cool.
      fire
        in
            the
              eyes.

COOL.

boats   boats echoing against
the rocks.

keep cool.

right out. flat.

firelight

EYELIGHT FIRELIGHT EYELIGHT.

its late.

LATER SO.

its later
later I'm told.
this is no all night party.
keep it strong.
up up up.

I don't want to see you.

DONE

down.

UP DOWN.
up up up.

I KNOW MY HEART FLIPPED.
i don't care.

look in my eyes

things beyond human speech
deep lighted bliss that has
no
begining middle or end.

up down.

time
to go
next door.
TIME TO GO

                    HOME.

        home.

            lameley led so.
        time to go

            to sleep.

            ho ho .   *perchance to dream*

    cold

            cold,

                its so cold
                    now

                        we came to pass
                    at the door.

            Just Before now.

    that the cold is in my bones
                        precious
                    cold how you feel

        how you feed.

                bones and all.

                        rattle.

            precious little in my blood.

    running cold.

                tortured goodbye.
        unsought you made it.

                you felt the fire.
                so did I.

    and the light.
            now well.
        flight fright.

                sight unbecoming.

truth not right.
   fucked up.

                        In the eye

out
     brief light.
     everyone knows its precious fire.

                          both legs
                          plonk
                                plonk.

BOTH FRIENDS.
KlinkK KlonK

                          at least then
                    I thought so.

                    friends.
                          ho ho.

friends in love
ho ho.

                                   love is precious

          firelight eyes

                    aeys.
                          fiery rich and.

I keep on having to go

both to that   sweet love

                    that sweet sight.

               unsought but found.

                          AND

               drink it in with my eyes.

to drift to the
                page again.

pale flame.

                                                    hey you

out there can you hear me .

                        can you see me

can you touch me.

                        no touch
                          no such
                        says he.

                PAIN NOW IN HIS EYES.

can't see

properly
        for the water.
just
            feeling
now
    not seeing
first
    the

        beautiful

            soul

    now

THE
heavy heart

oh
   WEEP WEEP
     unsteady on his feet

              of

                    emotions.

          SWIRLING WORLDS OF TEARS.
        unsteady action of love's eye

              HE
            slumbers stumbles.

stumbles like an

        ASLEEP WALKER NOT KNOWING.

bye

       he cries with his eyes.
         bye
       he says. I must go.

         BYE BYE.

B O N D S   O F   E M O T I O N S

yes

   bands of

        flags on the stars above.

                flashing

       in the street light.

yes I do.

                         I love you

I SWEAR I

            do.

              by the neon
                light.

I swear I do by the canal light.

                       yes I do I love you

I SWEAR I

     do.

        WALKING ALONG

              yes I do.

yes I do

        I love you.
      I swear I do from the
silence behind.

    yes

GLORIA
      of sight
            BEYOND.

and men   in the tongues of angels.

        and god.
      love is god.

                                        love is kind

a kind of love

            our kind of love

      kindred.

                                        there was no evil in mind

        there was no moving of
              mountains for we were

            NOT THINKING OF PROPHESISING

                  we had it then
                        that we had.
                  love.

        we had it then
              it was everything.
                        love.

not bad.
        love.

            not bad

            I never did look for it

                        then.

        you never did look for it then.

        it came.

      Wow Not bad Huh.

It Was True.

We

did not

we

just

we

just.

we just saw ourselves.

our eyes
our eyes.

our childrens eyes

eyes.

nc w ords.

did we speak

face to face.

love

flow

love.

face to face.

we
looked.

we

did

no more.

OH

we stood Open.

too.

our eyes

were open.

our Hearts

were open.

our
souls

were free.

at last.

THIS WAS IT.

our eyes were open
                              too.

          Hearts were open.

our souls were Free.
                          at last.

this was it.

          this is what   we

                    more than

                                        dreams of phantasies

                              o
                              f

                    B oo ks

                              o
                              f

                                        worlds of wisdom

are made of.
super-real.
sur-real
real.
real
all the way
the way.

          love Flowed

     and flowed.

on those

                on all
            around around
                us.

too.

                j
                 u s
                      t

            TWO.

that's all that's

left

                for the moment
                anyway.

                silence too.

            FEELINGS.

one way.

can I

                    just be
          blind.

    I say it was.

      I
    did
          love
                and all that.

THE SOUL

                of he
                    that has the HEART.

it's the   DREAM.

              IT'S THE ONE.

the one the one and only.

LIGHT
          that cannot be saved.

                from extinction.

      it   BURNS   sometimes still

bright.

          in the mind.

on low nights.

ALLways at NIGHT.

ha.

a n d the n i g h t is so cold.

so cold

so long so long

and you think
and you think.

god

I'm strong.

I should be dead

by now.

bye and bye now.

buried under the snow.

snow.

SNOWFLAKES.

buried under the
                    snowflakes.

        THE HEAVY

            all too HEAVY

                SNOW.

when you think the
                    words

        just

        just a love affair

        a   dream

all the same

                    hollowmen

I'd like to tell the real thing

        not just a picture on the wall
                    wouldn't you.

                                        just when it matters
yet
        all I do

                is Right

            is it right

Consolation

HERE AND NOW.

I

      I

                               *take them down to a place
by the river*

just a Night

     or hopefully just a few Hours.
     or even
     less.
     hopefully.

                              the boats go by

and you
    you want

  to fly back

    Back and you think

                             *you can spend the night
forever*

and He
    Fed you

juice and cheese

and a little meat.

and a lot of Stillness

and   LOVE.

and

     TENDERNESS.

     most of the Time

          rays of sun that illuminated

even

     if.

and he fed me all the Time.

and he told me that.

     just .

          that he had no love to give me

     that.

and he wants to travel with me.

          He touched Me

     again.

          only inside

shrinking away I think on the Other side.

god I must trust

he moves me and he's kind.

He leads me
        to a path
        there is air.
                        Shining.

                                    leaning out

and a honey

        honey.

        Just Tears now obscure. The words

as the
        thoughts

                        Flow in .

as the gates are laid open

        again.

                        to receive
        honey
        honey biscuits

just Honey biscuits.

                                    like the first time.

        a little bit Less

I must Trust My Heart.

and what I saw.
        and Stay a while.

my island
my love.

    waiting sadly
    not waiting
    not doing
    the LIGHT must be

Must come.

    Free
Again.

    free Him to walk. across the Water.

    saviour

Our Love.
    the water.

    he's Touched me.

           God.
    he's touched Me.

you can't disguise what you see.

he was wearing .

    GOODBYE

    leaning out of the

           Window.

is

    Love.

    looking down to the people.

below.

    it's difficult to carry on

having been and seen.

                You and I
high

                in
                the sky.

Bonded in love

                love

like an ax
pacified.

                        Oh you worlds of wisdom

come pass by Again

        so i hear your voices telling me it
                will be allright
                    right.

            Inside.

no letters says

        I

                not one.
then the Joy took me back again
                    by my hand.
    some time ago.
 it was later.

        the bonds of love
                or so I thought.

LOVER.

just love or lover./
   oh

I heard your voice again.

my friends

say they know

how I feel.

and then

           I

      See you Again
and then
      all the worlds

sound the same

all goes by.

and

we

Push in to greet each

other.

or so I think.

cool on the other side.

you cool.

Play it Again.

maybe if you want you do.

Angels came.

to say.

anyway.

Around the man.

up the house
in the woods.

The Room in My Home.

home.

(pause reader pause)

(feel reader feel)

stay awhile.

again.

feel it.

again.

didn't you.

words of a language
you have never seen

before

on our own.

away

Again.

nay.

he read the

letter   while I watched

his eyes his HEART.

and mine by default.
his Eyes

In the Sun

EYES.

(pause)

another happy meeting

and then we ate.

just a
little cupboard.

by the   window.

the HEART

          was in his eye.

again

          could not tell me lies

      he

our

      love

          too demanding

lonely hunter.

      lonely ?
      hunter ?

oh the heart was in his eyes.

      again.

      it slipped away.

trying to reach to loving

          believing

    this was no magazine.
    no idle sotry
    with too much wine.

the LOVE was here Again.

welcome.

                    a bit sought.

but welcome.

                    anyway.

          again.

  now in the lump of bread.

his' food.

              like the lump in my eyes.

NOW.

            juice

      in my eyes

                dream.

              swiming again

this was the life

          the life.

    there was the little cheese.
    and the little bit of meat.

little well.

DELICATE

                    and he

my Hand slows
quitens
inthe presence
of a bid sigh.

ASHES.

                no tears
                no sniffles
                just a sigh
                again
                from my eye-heart.

                sigh goodbye.
                sat down opposite me

we looked a little

eye for eye.

a bit too curious to see

to see

if it will come again.

he SMILED.

in the dark

he could see.

and smiled

the room became his smile.

I smiled now   in his image.

Grows
VIVID amongst
the first ashes.
SNOWFLAKES.

covering the winter's sniff.

cold.

in the dark he smiled.

sound and
light .

STARDUST.

everywhere.

oh yeah.

I swear it was no plaything.

no spiders
no webs.

we really sang.

do you know

what

I mean.
just a little.

he was trying to hard to

see.

intellectually.

or so I told him.
this is what I thought

when

I laughed.

when he asked.

well ?

just the

there were candles I forgot.
was it

one or two ?

i can't remember.

this time.

its all here.

ah

it was so god given.

creating Love

        generating LOVE

   making Love.

love love do you hear. born again love .not dead

not yet.
not prejudiced
not hating
not converting

               people smile and I say

even though even though

               I'm the lucky one

   now a smile

ALL ok now now its all SMILES.

i hope on your face DEAR READER

      for the good
      for the beautiful
      for the feeling

   that swells inside.

open

    those

       places
           those
             palaces
just

   you

      and

          I

now I see it all again

      even though.

    we were so IN love

beyond love's measurement.

         and after

    or was it
    before.

              photographing in our mind

all about love.
      LOVE just

          was

    there.

                              no

                    pinpoint

           place

or time then.

just the FORCE of love,

                                        no mysteries now

           all about

                    love

           all about   even now

                    love

                    even though

                         a chain of love.

LIFE sat.

           sat there on a tree stump.

                    in a middle of a field.

           alone.

he looked up.

                    and saw

                         love.

           silently

the WIDE
eyes.

           stranger to him.

strange
                    to him.

                                    LOVE.

        a stranger to him.

singing.

                                                    homeward sailor

                    I'm thinking

about the day
            the day in

                    Neightmegen

                                            the songs of the sailor
                                            homeward sailor
                                            homeward sailor

                            hurry
love is waiting.

        hurry life.

                    and later on.

                            the JOY
            sank to his knees.

LIGHT

        of the sun.

                    shove so.
sure so.

bright

its tiny pulses .

he spoke
he laughed
he thought
he played
he rejoiced

DEEP

deep in his heart.

over backwards.

and forward too.

FOREVER.

it is so beautiful.

I can't believe

the growth in my eye.

looking up from one knee
to the heaven above.

Sometimes.

now he

EYED

with his hands   weary

Heavy

homeward bound
running from reason

running from love.
    eyes that see
                    not what is to see and
seen
        smokey
                reaching for a last

                                reaching for a lost smile

stranded
        looking away now for a
                who cares what

oh love you and I grow faint. the
ravines are to cold. the snow is piled
to high above the earth to see. ashes. where
is my eye   now

                                to melt the darkness in my sou

        the   Snowing Lane

                                how you suffered for

        me   the

                                dark lands

And   the   brIght

lands to see.   You

above steal the light from the past.
cast it on the future. our love is
true. reflection. on as
beautiful as you.
reflection.

and   you want   him
        to come.

                                to travel with

and you don't touch him and you don't move.

so you go so you sing.

I wish I could see you
like the first time

but
ah but
I do you   see.
        room sitting
        one.   Another
look
eye
look
feel
be.
me.
be.
Being.
        on the third
        stroke.
we   sailed   across
his   home.
his   family.
his   home.
his   room.
his bed.
ah life
Love.
        still   sitting
there.
all there.

slow.
meat.
feet.
we watched the paintings
Pass by.
the cars.
Again.
        passing by.
                only once
did an angry tenderless voice say.
See for yourself.
can't you.
        ah well.
                or words to that effect.
did he know then the meaning now.
        it somehow slipped out.

        we walked.   again.

to the train.
riding without a hitch.
first.

                AND THEN
a cup of coffee
warmth by the smoke by

the smoke.

face   to   face.

AGAIN.

body face body
warmth
eye.
FELT it.

he touched me gently then.
gently.
with such tenderness
and protection
I
I
        believe
shrank back.
                        maybe this is for real.
                        or
did I remember   the time some time ago.

when I did the SAME.
and he
he .
shrugged off the touching tender hand.
no   one

                was looking.

                no one CARED.

                it was a GOOD time
then.

it was a good time then.

I can recall.
the times we just looked again.

thrice now.

in different forms.

who   but   GOD

knows love.   FLOWS

tripple echo.
it is done.
we have won.
we had a joint.
he MADE them.
a lover's hand
hand.
gently.
advising.

he   KNEW   how.

pocket it.

later.

use it.

later too

we did.

ashes form from the smoke.
snowflakes from the fire.

another flight home.

time and time and time

AGAIN
gentlemen
TIME to go

say goodbye.
        sod.
don't look back.
                    if he does.
then   there is   nothing.
did   he.   no.
just walked on.   as if.
he did not care.

        he did.

just other things now.
who cares.

time time time

gentlemen.

        drink up.   hear the words.

next time.

remember me
            and

love

and him.

            ok reader now read on.

oh standing at the wall.

emanations.

nice and easy.

penthouse view.

                                        high flying adored

sister of the phantasy.

            so high
            so adored

                                        all this yours

                you called

                                        someone on top of the world

by tele first to the sister of the phantasy

later.

gone.

then.

come again.

                    you don't care

to call.

me.

        otherwise.

                    now its ok.

local   guy makes good.

                    makes good.

he   talks to me and I feel
                    he
does   not   want to stop.

just
lonely.

                    all the rest
gone   now.

he   wants to   talk.

well
nothing bad in that.
after
all I
just wrote.

and talk and talk.

            just   talk.
more than.

            he tells me things.
ordinary things.

he has given up his studies now.

            records.

                    a new age.
anyway.

and I am just well
talking.

                                    that's all I was doing
            and we say.

or   rather   I.

                                    say goodbye.

I feel his tremor.

bless his sister of the phantasy.
                        coming
            to
visit.

me

        bless

                        and now.

no

                any

        many

                        letters

words

                        and now

                with

well

                heart in waiting.

well

it

alone

alone

again

I

together

beside

GROW

LOVE

again

alone

again

just

two

eyes

together again

together again

Note by the Publisher 2013

Mæg ic be me sylfum	I can make a true song
soðgied wrecan,	about me myself,

The Seafarer, date unknown.(Approximate translation of the old English)

Song, established in 2013 is an imprint of a new publication house, a division of Song of the Wild Swan Ltd.

It publishes any writings from anyone who has a song.

Song also participates in the BEL (Barter Exchange Levy) Price System.

List of Selected Works by orde

Song, November 2013
Areas of classification may overlap

Books

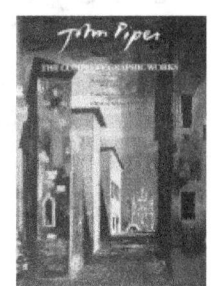

1   *John Piper – The Complete Graphic Works: A
       Catalogue Raisonné 1923-1983.* Compiled and
       edited by Orde Levinson. Faber & Faber,
       1988.

2   *I Was Lonelyness: The Complete Graphic Works
       of John Muafangejo 1968-1987.* Struik
       Winchester, 1992. Foreword by Archbishop
       Desmond Tutu. Contributing essays from:
       Olga Levinson (The Life and Art of John
       Muafangejo); Edward Lucie-Smith (John
       Muafangejo); Pat Gilmour (On Not Being a
       Political Artist); Orde Levinson (John
       Muafangejo, Cubism and Traditional African

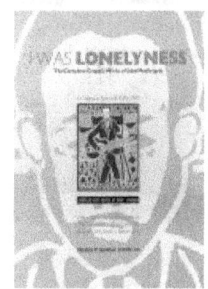

       Art); Olga Levinson (The Historical
       Development of Art in Namibia) and Steven
       Sack (The Rorke's Drift Art and Craft
       Centre) and all Muafangejo's Interviews,
       Statements and published conversations.

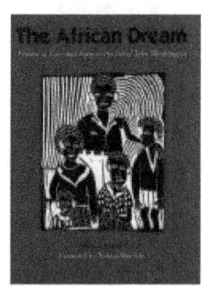

3   *The African Dream – Visions of Love and
       Sorrow. The Art Of John Muafangejo.* Thames
       and Hudson, 1993. Foreword by Nelson
       Mandela.

4   *Quality and Experiment. The Prints of John
       Piper – A Catalogue Raisonné.* Lund
       Humphries, 1996.

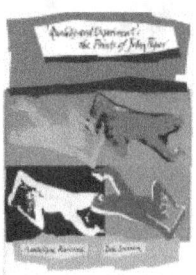

5   *The Prints of John Piper – A Catalogue Raisonné
       1921-1991.* Lund Humphries, 2010.
       Contributing essays: Introduction (Orde
       Levinson); Experiment and Quality (Orde
       Levinson); Subject and Technique in Piper's
       Printmaking (David Fraser Jenkins); Working
       with Printers (John Piper).

6 *Hitting the Nail on the Head – The Complete Written Works of John Piper 1913-1992.* An estimated three volumes with contributing essays by various authors (tba). Scheduled for publication 2014/5.

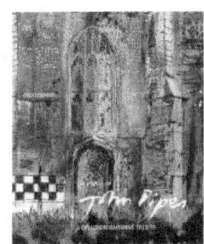

7 *Delights and Aphorisms, selected writings of John Piper.* Scheduled for publication 2014-5.

8 *Daniel Henry Kahnweiler: A bibliography.* Scheduled for publication 2014.

9 *The Life and Work of Daniel Henry Kahnweiler: A critical evaluation.* Originally part of the D. Phil. Study at Magdalen College, Oxford University. Scheduled for publication 2015.

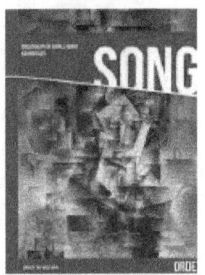

10 *The Complete Writings of Daniel Henry Kahnweiler.* Three volumes. Scheduled for publication 2015-6.

Conversations and interviews

11 *orde's Conversations with Henry Moore.* Henry Moore talks about influences, the artists he likes, his work and life in general. Available as eBook 2013 Book published by Song 2014

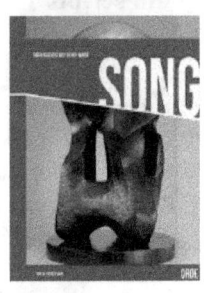

12 *Orde's Conversations with Richard Sorabji (videoed)* in progress,. Richard Sorabji in thought and in person is brought to us in a unique experiment where orde has selected friends from each decade to converse with him. Completed to date are Louis Hynes (age 10); Laurence Hutton-Smith (age 20); Richard Kuziara (age 37); Lisa Hammond-Marty (age 40-50); Jeremy Rowe (age 50-58); Marianne Talbot (age 58--68) Joanna Foster (age 68-80). Available as video, eBook and book. Scheduled publication 2015.

13 *Talking to Solly Irwin (videoed)*
Schedule publication as eBook and book 2014-5,

Films

14 *Essences*. Independent production
produced by orde under the inspiration of
Straub and Huillet. A contemplative
mood piece starring Richard E. Grant
and Kiki Savejan
Director/script/editor: orde
Cast: Richard E Grant, Kiki Savejan
Running Time: 40 minutes/colour
Date Completed: 1983
(Image: Scene Shot from Essences by orde.)

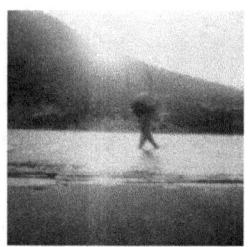

15 Ÿ
Director/script/editor: orde
Cast: Richard E Grant
Running time:16 minutes/colour
Date Completed: c.1987.

Film scripts

16 *The Judgment of Shylock*. In progress.

In fermentation/digestion

17 *The Inventors dilemma*. A novel?
18 *Five Fingers are not the same*. A novel?
19 *Turquoise*. A love story.
20 *The Weather of myself*. A philosophical book/diary.
21 *The Human Tragedy*. A true story, novel/poem?

Music

22 *I am here thank you please, a musical
composition*. Contains an introduction on
classical and romantic by orde.
Available 2014 as eBook and book (published
by Song.

23 *Le Bordel Philosophique*. A musical composition
with 5 contemporary composers (George
Barton, Sam Fernando, Cheryl Francis-Hoad, Simon Roth, Jaime
Wolfson). A composition based on a poem, which is based on a
painting to reach a musical gesamtkunstwerk for our era.
Scheduled for completion 2014.

Plays

24   *Forcible Love.* A play based on the life of John
           Muafangejo.

25   *Forcible Love (NTN version).* A musical on the
           life of John Muafangejo - premiered at the
           National Theatre, Windhoek, Namibia for the
           Independence Celebrations. Includes reviews.
           Available 2014 as eBook and book (published
           by Song)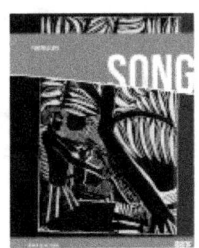

26   *The Rialto Dialogues.* Described as a
           revolutionary work about the Merchant of
           Venice by William Shakespeare. It includes the
           entire work uncut but introduces 4 new
           characters to open a meaning and channel to
           one of Shakespeare's greatest plays.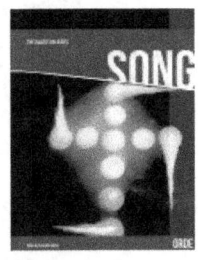
           Available 2014 as eBook and book (published
           by Song)

27   *Shylock the Magnificent.* A play 13 years after
           the Trial Scene of the Merchant of Venice by Shakespeare.
           Available 2014 as eBook and book (published by Song)
           See also The Soul's Heritage under poems.

Poems

28   *Miscellaneous poems.* Short poems found over
           the years.
           Available 2014 as eBook and book.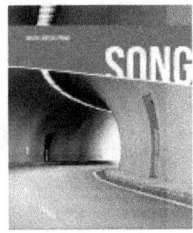

29   *The Love song of D. Adolph Hitler.* In progress.
30   *Der Tod Des Miguel.* In progress

31   *Les Dem.* About Picasso's painting *Les Demoiselles D'Avignon,*
           includes essay on *Les Dem* by Professor Andrew Laird.
           Available 2014 as eBook and book (published by Song).

32   *Ndilapa Nkosi.* A lyrical comedy, first part of *The Soul's Heritage,* a
           trilogy, a landmark work described by Samuel Beckett as a
           'moving feat'. Includes reviews and responses from various persons
           including Beckett.

Available 2014 as eBook and book (published
by Song).

33   *Antomat Diplony of the Orb.* An epic comedy,
in progress, second part of The Soul's
Heritage, a trilogy.

34   *The Argonauta Vineyard.* A tragic comedy, in
progress, third part of The Soul's Heritage, a
trilogy.

35   *Parlez à Voir.*
Available 2014 as eBook and book (published
by Song).

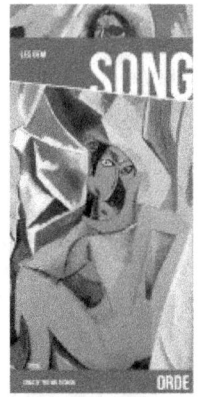

36   *Flying strongly on one wing.*
Available 2014 as eBook and book (published
by Song).

37   *Snowflakes and Ashes.*
Available 2014 as eBook and book (published
by Song).

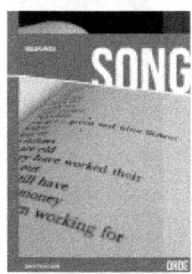

Reviews and articles

38   A number of articles and reviews exist and are
being collated.

39   *Art, An Adaptive Function?*
Encyclopaedia of Evolution Mark Pagel
(Editor-in-Chief), Oxford University Press,
2002. (365 articles from 330 different
authors).

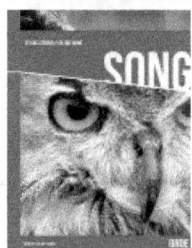

Visual works

Drawings, paintings, photography, prints,
sculptures
Please see www.orde.info

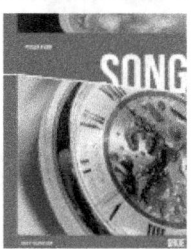